**Editor**
Gisela Lee, M.A.

**Managing Editor**
Karen Goldfluss, M.S. Ed.

**Editor-in-Chief**
Sharon Coan, M.S. Ed.

**Cover Artist**
Barb Lorseyedi

**Art Manager**
Kevin Barnes

**Art Director**
CJae Froshay

**Imaging**
Craig Gunnell

**Product Manager**
Phil Garcia

**Publisher**
Mary D. Smith, M.S. Ed.

Practice Makes Perfect

# Place Value

## GRADE 2

Includes practice
for Standardized Tests

**Author**

*Mary Rosenberg*

*Teacher Created Resources, Inc.*
12621 Western Avenue
Garden Grove, CA 92841
www.teachercreated.com

8602-1

©200                                      *Inc.*

D1502336

# Table of Contents

# Introduction

The old adage "practice makes perfect" can really hold true for your child and his or her education. The more practice and exposure your child has with concepts being taught in school, the more success he or she is likely to find. For many parents, knowing how to help their children can be frustrating because the resources may not be readily available. As a parent, it is also difficult to know where to focus your efforts so that the extra practice your child receives at home supports what he or she is learning in school.

This book has been designed to help parents and teachers reinforce basic skills with children. *Practice Makes Perfect: Place Value* reviews basic math skills for children in grade 2. While it would be impossible to include all concepts taught in grade 2 in this book, the following basic objectives are reinforced through practice exercises. These objectives support math standards established on a district, state, or national level. (Refer to the Table of Contents for specific objectives of each practice page.)

- skip counting by 5s, 10s, 25s, 50s, and 100s
- odd and even numbers
- counting money
- solving word problems
- lace value to the hundreds
- identifying and writing numbers using only numbers, numbers and words, and only words
- comparing numbers using the symbols >, <, and =
- using place value blocks to solve problems

- adding and subtracting to the hundreds with and without regrouping
- using a chart to solve a problem
- solving 3-digit math problems
- identifying the number that comes before, in the middle, and after
- identifying the value of a number based upon its place
- solving place value riddles
- working with fractions

There are 36 practice pages. (**Note:** Have children show all work where computation is necessary to solve a problem.) Following the practice pages are six test practices. These provide children with multiple-choice test items to help prepare them for standardized tests administered in schools. To correct the test pages and the practice pages in this book, use the answer key provided on pages 47 and 48.

## How to Make the Most of This Book

Here are some useful ideas for optimizing the practice pages in this book:

- Set aside a specific place in your home to work on the practice pages. Keep it neat and tidy with materials on hand.
- Set up a certain time of day to work on the practice pages. This will establish consistency. Look for times in your day or week that are less hectic and more conducive to practicing skills.
- Keep all practice sessions with your child positive and more constructive. If your child is having difficulty understanding what to do or how to get started, work through the first problem with him or her.
- Review the work your child has done. This serves as reinforcement and provides further practice.
- Pay attention to the areas in which your child has the most difficulty. Provide extra guidance and exercises in those areas. Allowing children to use drawings and manipulatives, such as coins, tiles, game markers, or flash cards, can help them grasp difficult concepts more easily.

# Practice 1

Draw the place value blocks for each number.

| | |
|---|---|
| **1.** 5 | 4 |
| **2.** 3 | 1 |
| **3.** 9 | 6 |
| **4.** 0 | 8 |
| **5.** 7 | 2 |

Compare the two numbers. Circle the one that is larger.

| | | |
|---|---|---|
| **11.** | 5 | 8 |
| **12.** | 5 | 2 |
| **13.** | 1 | 5 |
| **14.** | 6 | 10 |
| **15.** | 4 | 3 |
| **16.** | 7 | 0 |
| **17.** | 9 | 7 |
| **18.** | 2 | 1 |
| **19.** | 8 | 4 |
| **20.** | 0 | 6 |
| **21.** | 4 | 5 |
| **22.** | 3 | 7 |

Compare the two numbers. Circle the one that is less.

| | | |
|---|---|---|
| **23.** | 9 | 10 |
| **24.** | 2 | 7 |
| **25.** | 7 | 6 |
| **26.** | 2 | 5 |
| **27.** | 4 | 5 |
| **28.** | 9 | 3 |
| **29.** | 9 | 0 |
| **30.** | 7 | 3 |
| **31.** | 1 | 0 |
| **32.** | 10 | 1 |
| **33.** | 3 | 5 |
| **34.** | 5 | 6 |

 #8602 Practice Makes Perfect: Place Value

# Practice 2

Circle sets of ten. Write the number of tens and ones.

| Example: | Tens | Ones |
|---|---|---|
| ☆☆☆☆☆☆☆☆☆☆☆☆☆ | 1 | 3 |

1. ☆☆☆☆☆☆☆☆☆☆☆☆☆
   ☆☆☆

   | Tens | Ones |
   |---|---|

2. ☆☆☆☆☆☆☆☆☆☆☆☆☆
   ☆

   | Tens | Ones |
   |---|---|

3. ☆☆☆☆☆☆☆☆☆☆☆☆☆
   ☆☆☆☆☆☆☆☆☆☆☆

   | Tens | Ones |
   |---|---|

4. ☆☆☆☆☆☆☆☆☆☆☆☆☆
   ☆☆☆☆☆☆☆☆

   | Tens | Ones |
   |---|---|

5. ☆☆☆☆☆☆☆☆☆

   | Tens | Ones |
   |---|---|

6. ☆☆☆☆☆☆☆☆☆☆☆☆

   | Tens | Ones |
   |---|---|

7. ☆☆☆☆☆☆☆☆☆☆☆☆☆☆☆☆☆☆

   | Tens | Ones |
   |---|---|

8. ☆☆☆☆☆☆☆☆

   | Tens | Ones |
   |---|---|

# Practice 3

Write the number of tens.

**1.**

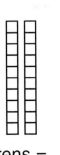

____ tens = _____

**5.**

____ ten = _____

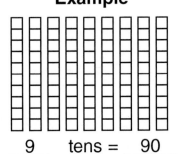

| **Example** |
|---|

____9____ tens = ____90____

**2.**

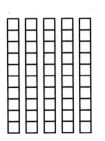

____ tens = _____

**6.**

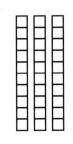

____ tens = _____

Write the number.

**9.** eleven _____

**10.** twelve _____

**11.** thirteen _____

**12.** fourteen _____

**13.** fifteen _____

**14.** sixteen _____

**3.**

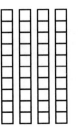

____ tens = _____

**7.**

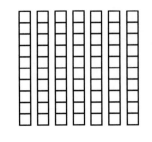

____ tens = _____

**15.** seventeen _____

**16.** eighteen _____

**17.** nineteen _____

**18.** twenty _____

**19.** twenty-five _____

**20.** thirty _____

**21.** forty _____

**4.**

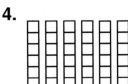

____ tens = _____

**8.**

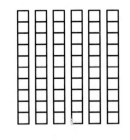

____ tens = _____

**22.** fifty _____

**23.** sixty _____

**24.** seventy _____

**25.** seventy-five _____

**26.** eighty _____

**27.** ninety _____

**28.** one hundred _____

# Practice 4

Write the number of tens and ones.

**Example**

| Tens | Ones |
|------|------|
| 3 | 8 |

_38_

**1.**

| Tens | Ones |
|------|------|
|  |  |

_____

**2.**

| Tens | Ones |
|------|------|
|  |  |

_____

**3.**

| Tens | Ones |
|------|------|
|  |  |

_____

**4.**

| Tens | Ones |
|------|------|
|  |  |

_____

**5.**

| Tens | Ones |
|------|------|
|  |  |

_____

**6.**

| Tens | Ones |
|------|------|
|  |  |

_____

**7.**

| Tens | Ones |
|------|------|
|  |  |

_____

**8.**

| Tens | Ones |
|------|------|
|  |  |

_____

**9.**

| Tens | Ones |
|------|------|
|  |  |

_____

**10.**

| Tens | Ones |
|------|------|
|  |  |

_____

**11.**

| Tens | Ones |
|------|------|
|  |  |

_____

# Practice 5

## Write the number of tens and ones.

**Example**

| Tens | Ones |
|------|------|
| 6 | 7 |

67

**1.**

| Tens | Ones |
|------|------|
|  |  |

_____

**2.**

| Tens | Ones |
|------|------|
|  |  |

_____

**3.**

| Tens | Ones |
|------|------|
|  |  |

_____

**4.**

| Tens | Ones |
|------|------|
|  |  |

_____

**5.**

| Tens | Ones |
|------|------|
|  |  |

_____

**6.**

| Tens | Ones |
|------|------|
|  |  |

_____

**7.**

| Tens | Ones |
|------|------|
|  |  |

_____

**8.**

| Tens | Ones |
|------|------|
|  |  |

_____

**9.**

| Tens | Ones |
|------|------|
|  |  |

_____

**10.**

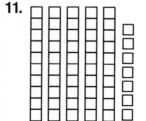

| Tens | Ones |
|------|------|
|  |  |

_____

**11.**

| Tens | Ones |
|------|------|
|  |  |

_____

# Practice 6

Use the symbols: > (greater than), < (less than), or = (equal to) to compare each set of numbers.

**1.**  ◯ 32

**2.** 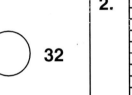 ◯ 26

**3.** 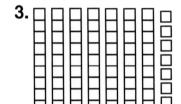 ◯ 88

**4.** 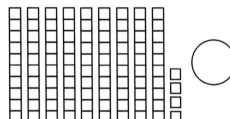 ◯ 62

**5.** 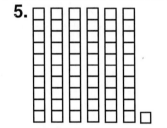 ◯ 62

**6.** 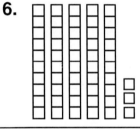 ◯ 55

**7.**  ◯ 19

**8.** 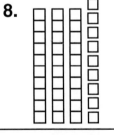 ◯ 93

**9.** ◯ 71

**10.** ◯ 44

**11.**  ◯ 55

**12.** 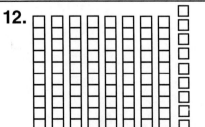 ◯ 97

# Practice 7

Write the number.

**Example: seventy-three = 73**

**1.** twenty-three = _____    **6.** ninety-eight = _____    **11.** eighty-five = _____

**2.** fourteen = _____    **7.** forty-four = _____    **12.** ten = _____

**3.** thirty-nine = _____    **8.** fifty-three = _____    **13.** seventeen = _____

**4.** thirty-seven = _____    **9.** seventy = _____    **14.** ninety-four = _____

**5.** sixty-nine = _____    **10.** eighty-one = _____    **15.** forty-one = _____

Write the following in expanded notation.

**Examples: 55 = 50 + 5        seventy-one = 70 + 1**

**16.** 28 = _____ + _____    **21.** seventy-three = _____ + _____

**17.** 16 = _____ + _____    **22.** fifteen = _____ + _____

**18.** 61 = _____ + _____    **23.** thirty = _____ + _____

**19.** 83 = _____ + _____    **24.** eighty-two = _____ + _____

**20.** 40 = _____ + _____    **25.** fifty-five = _____ + _____

Write the following as words.

**Example: 21 = twenty-one**

**26.** 22 = _____    **31.** 81 = _____

**27.** 56 = _____    **32.** 44 = _____

**28.** 92 = _____    **33.** 68 = _____

**29.** 46 = _____    **34.** 35 = _____

**30.** 37 = _____    **35.** 10 = _____

# Practice 8

Solve each problem.

| | | |
|---|---|---|
| **1.** 10<br>+ 81 | **2.** 22<br>+ 45 | **3.** 47<br>+ 41 |

**4.** 10
+ 10

**5.** 23
+ 31

**6.** 21
+ 13

**7.** 55
+ 14

**8.** 51
+ 38

**9.** 18
+ 31

**10.** 41
+ 52

**11.** 10
+ 59

**12.** 18
+ 60

**13.** 12
+ 44

**14.** 21
+ 13

**15.** 14
+ 21

**16.** 21
+ 73

**17.** 51
+ 38

**18.** 21
+ 44

**19.** 18
+ 50

**20.** 65
+ 31

# Practice 9

Solve each problem.

1.  10
    + 81

2.  42
    + 42

3.  57
    + 30

4.  23
    + 75

5.  54
    + 11

6.  15
    + 72

7.  35
    + 31

8.  68
    + 10

9.  11
    + 67

10. 12
    + 20

11. 61
    + 18

12. 86
    + 10

13. 60
    + 17

14. 36
    + 41

15. 13
    + 43

16. 25
    + 40

17. 38
    + 61

18. 53
    + 12

19. 19
    + 70

20. 46
    + 43

# Practice 10

Solve each problem.

| | | |
|---|---|---|
| **1.**   34<br>+ 59 | **2.**   74<br>+ 19 | **3.**   53<br>+ 17 |

| | | |
|---|---|---|
| **4.**   13<br>+ 79 | **5.**   26<br>+  8 | **6.**   15<br>+ 65 |

| | | |
|---|---|---|
| **7.**   68<br>+ 13 | **8.**   77<br>+ 18 | **9.**   13<br>+ 57 |

| | | |
|---|---|---|
| **10.** 56<br>+ 26 | **11.** 27<br>+ 44 | **12.** 16<br>+ 46 |

# Practice 11

Solve each problem.

| | | | | |
|---|---|---|---|---|
| **1.**  35<br>+ 55 | **2.**  17<br>+ 74 | **3.**  16<br>+ 65 | **4.**  43<br>+ 49 | **5.**  72<br>+ 19 |

| | | | | |
|---|---|---|---|---|
| **6.**  57<br>+ 16 | **7.**  18<br>+ 77 | **8.**  68<br>+ 26 | **9.**  28<br>+ 35 | **10.** 76<br>+ 18 |

| | | | | |
|---|---|---|---|---|
| **11.** 74<br>+ 19 | **12.** 34<br>+ 57 | **13.** 26<br>+ 29 | **14.** 17<br>+ 77 | **15.** 65<br>+ 28 |

| | | | | |
|---|---|---|---|---|
| **16.** 23<br>+ 49 | **17.** 28<br>+ 56 | **18.** 67<br>+ 24 | **19.** 16<br>+ 26 | **20.** 66<br>+ 15 |

# Practice 12 ꙮ ꙮ ꙮ ꙮ ꙮ ꙮ ꙮ ꙮ ꙮ ꙮ ꙮ ꙮ ꙮ ꙮ

Solve each word problem.

1. There are 8 boys and 12 girls in Juan's class.
   How many students in all? _____

2. Seventeen first grade classes and 16 second grade classes went on a field trip. How many classes in all?_____

3. There were 18 third graders and 24 fourth graders in the cafeteria.
   How many students in all? _____

4. On the playground 25 students were playing soccer and 28 students were playing basketball. How many students were playing in all?_____

5. In the library there were 13 students reading books and 19 students checking out books. How many students in all?_____

6. After school, 37 students walked home and 45 students rode the bus.
   How many students in all? _____

7. Mike sold 34 bottles of juice and 47 bottles of milk.
   How many drinks did he sell in all?_____

8. Joan sold 12 bags of peanuts and 39 bags of popcorn.
   How many bags did Joan sell in all? _____

9. Tom sold 17 hot dogs and 29 hamburgers.
   How many items did Tom sell in all? _____

10. Kelly sold 39 cupcakes and 24 ice cream cones.
    How many desserts did Kelly sell in all? _____

# Practice 13

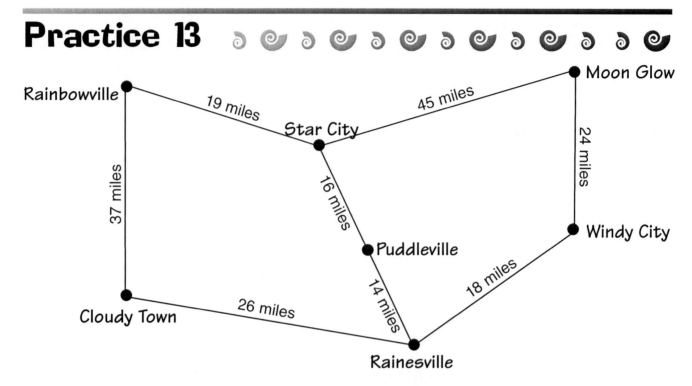

Find the number of miles going through the fewest.

**Ex:** Rainbowville to Moon Glow   19 + 45 = 64 miles

**1.** Rainbowville to Puddleville   _____

**2.** Star City to Cloudy Town   _____

**3.** Moon Glow to Rainbowville   _____

**4.** Cloudy Town to Puddleville   _____

**5.** Rainbowville to Rainesville   _____

**6.** Moon Glow to Puddleville   _____

**7.** Star City to Windy City   _____

**8.** Cloudy Town to Windy City   _____

**9.** Rainesville to Moon Glow   _____

Use the symbols > (greater than), < (less than), or = (equal to) to compare the distances.

**10.** Rainbowville to Cloudy Town   ◯   Star City to Moon Glow

**11.** Windy City to Rainesville   ◯   Cloudy Town to Rainesville

**12.** Rainbowville to Star City   ◯   Windy City to Moon Glow

**13.** Star City to Puddleville   ◯   Rainesville to Cloudy Town

# Practice 14

Solve each problem.

1.  68
  − 32

2.  78
  − 12

3.  48
  − 11

4.  69
  − 13

5.  64
  − 31

6.  57
  − 10

7.  97
  − 92

8.  84
  − 82

9.  48
  − 12

10. 99
  − 38

11. 95
  − 54

12. 75
  − 15

13. 53
  − 53

14. 66
  − 16

15. 87
  − 25

16.

| − 6 | |
|-----|---|
| 97 | |
| 36 | |
| 67 | |
| 89 | |
| 48 | |
| 17 | |

17.

| − 2 | |
|-----|---|
| 85 | |
| 74 | |
| 27 | |
| 43 | |
| 15 | |
| 53 | |

18.

| − 1 | |
|-----|---|
| 22 | |
| 91 | |
| 11 | |
| 14 | |
| 86 | |
| 31 | |

# Practice 15

Solve each problem.

1. 68
   − 32
   _____

4. 69
   − 13
   _____

7. 97
   − 92
   _____

10. 99
    − 38
    _____

2. 78
   − 12
   _____

5. 64
   − 31
   _____

8. 84
   − 82
   _____

11. 95
    − 54
    _____

3. 48
   − 11
   _____

6. 57
   − 10
   _____

9. 48
   − 12
   _____

12. 75
    − 15
    _____

13. Tia had 96¢.  She spent 60¢ buying a new folder.
    How much money does Tia have left?_____

14. Daniel had 88¢.  He spent 77¢ buying a school pennant.
    How much money does Daniel have left?_____

15. Josie had 94¢.  She spent 21¢ buying an eraser.
    How much money does Josie have left?_____

16. Aaron had 53¢.  He spent 11¢ buying a baseball card.
    How much money does Aaron have left?_____

17. Shane had 86¢.  He spent 31¢ buying a pen.
    How much money does Shane have left?_____

18. Diana had 57¢.  She spent 17¢ buying a bookmark.
    How much money does Diana have left?_____

# Practice 16

Solve each problem.

| | | | | |
|---|---|---|---|---|
| **1.**   91<br>  − 42 | **2.**   67<br>  − 58 | **3.**   72<br>  − 53 | **4.**   84<br>  − 19 | **5.**   80<br>  − 17 |
| **6.**   33<br>  − 15 | **7.**   54<br>  − 19 | **8.**   65<br>  − 47 | **9.**   93<br>  − 86 | **10.**   83<br>  − 39 |
| **11.**   85<br>  − 28 | **12.**   72<br>  − 18 | **13.**   41<br>  − 23 | **14.**   54<br>  − 16 | **15.**   63<br>  − 37 |
| **16.**   66<br>  − 39 | **17.**   91<br>  − 18 | **18.**   64<br>  − 47 | **19.**   90<br>  − 74 | **20.**   82<br>  − 25 |

# Practice 17

Solve each problem. Add to check.

1.   $\begin{array}{r} 83 \\ -\ 47 \\ \hline \end{array}$

2.   $\begin{array}{r} 80 \\ -\ 59 \\ \hline \end{array}$

3.   $\begin{array}{r} 50 \\ -\ 31 \\ \hline \end{array}$

4.   $\begin{array}{r} 56 \\ -\ 19 \\ \hline \end{array}$

5.   $\begin{array}{r} 32 \\ -\ 13 \\ \hline \end{array}$

6.   $\begin{array}{r} 94 \\ -\ 67 \\ \hline \end{array}$

7.   $\begin{array}{r} 88 \\ -\ 79 \\ \hline \end{array}$

8.   $\begin{array}{r} 63 \\ -\ 56 \\ \hline \end{array}$

9.   $\begin{array}{r} 60 \\ -\ 33 \\ \hline \end{array}$

10.   $\begin{array}{r} 41 \\ -\ 17 \\ \hline \end{array}$

11.   $\begin{array}{r} 95 \\ -\ 69 \\ \hline \end{array}$

12.   $\begin{array}{r} 63 \\ -\ 27 \\ \hline \end{array}$

13.   $\begin{array}{r} 81 \\ -\ 44 \\ \hline \end{array}$

14.   $\begin{array}{r} 25 \\ -\ 16 \\ \hline \end{array}$

15.   $\begin{array}{r} 90 \\ -\ 75 \\ \hline \end{array}$

# Practice 18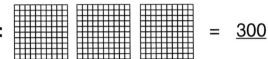

Write the number of hundreds.

**Example :** = 300

1. = _____

2. = _____

3. = _____

4. = _____

5. = _____

6. = _____

7. = _____

8. = _____

# Practice 19

Write the number.

### Example

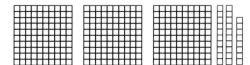 3 hundreds + 2 tens + 8 ones = 300 + 20 + 8 = 328

1.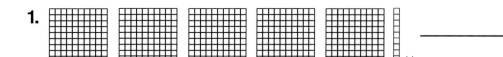

2. _____

3.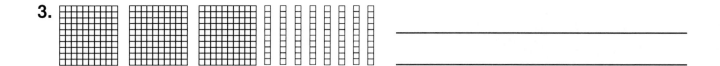

4. _____

5.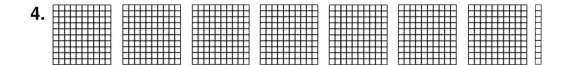

6.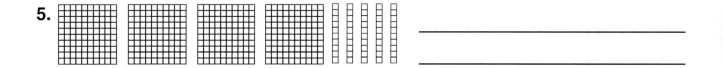

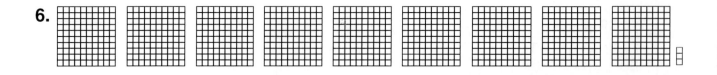

# Practice 20

Write the number.

1. 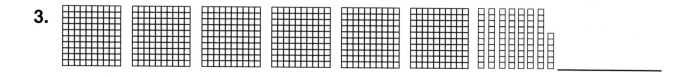 _____

2. _____

3. _____

4. _____

5. _____

6. _____

# Practice 21

Write the place value for each circled digit.

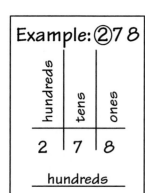

Example: ②78

|          |      |      |
| hundreds | tens | ones |
|    2     |  7   |  8   |

hundreds

**1.** 2 2 ⑥

_____

**2.** 1 ⑧ 6

_____

**3.** 1 1 ⓪

_____

**4.** 7 9 ④

_____

**5.** ④ 0 1

_____

**6.** 6 3 ⑧

_____

Circle the largest digit.  Write the place value of the largest digit on the line.

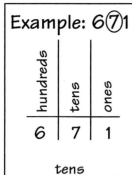

Example: 6⑦1

|          |      |      |
| hundreds | tens | ones |
|    6     |  7   |  1   |

tens

**7.**  815

_____

**8.**  658

_____

**9.**  263

_____

**10.**  983

_____

**11.**  598

_____

**12.**  947

_____

Circle the larger number.  Write the place value of the two digits compared in order to find the larger number.

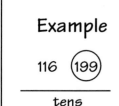

Example

116  ⑲⑼⑼

_____
tens

**13.** 810  944

_____

**14.**  375  301

_____

**15.**  341  932

_____

**16.** 261  851

_____

**17.**  677  676

_____

**18.**  199  108

_____

# Practice 22

Solve each problem.

| | | | | | |
|---|---|---|---|---|---|
| **1.** 300 <br> + 100 | **2.** 100 <br> + 800 | **3.** 600 <br> − 500 | **4.** 900 <br> − 700 | **5.** 500 <br> − 200 | **6.** 800 <br> − 800 |

| | | | | | |
|---|---|---|---|---|---|
| **7.** 700 <br> − 300 | **8.** 200 <br> + 400 | **9.** 800 <br> − 600 | **10.** 900 <br> − 800 | **11.** 900 <br> − 700 | **12.** 200 <br> + 200 |

Compare each set of numbers using the symbols > (greater than), < (less than), or = (equal to).

**13.** 100 + 700 ◯ 800

**14.** 400 + 400 ◯ 100

**15.** 400 + 400 ◯ 300

**16.** 900 + 300 ◯ 600

**17.** 100 + 800 ◯ 300

**18.** 900 + 600 ◯ 300

**19.** 600 + 300 ◯ 500

**20.** 600 + 400 ◯ 100

**21.** 500 + 300 ◯ 700

**22.** 100 + 300 ◯ 400

**23.** 900 + 800 ◯ 600

**24.** 800 + 300 ◯ 400

# Practice 23 ꙮ ꙮ ꙮ ꙮ ꙮ ꙮ ꙮ ꙮ ꙮ ꙮ ꙮ ꙮ ꙮ ꙮ

Write the number.

**Example:** one hundred sixty-nine  169

1. seven hundred seventy-eight _____
2. four hundred six  _____
3. two hundred thirty-three  _____
4. four hundred ninety-one  _____
5. two hundred forty-seven  _____

6. three hundred ninety-six  _____
7. five hundred sixty-four  _____
8. one hundred twenty-five  _____
9. nine hundred eighty-seven  _____
10. six hundred ninety-nine  _____

Write the following in expanded notation.

**Example:** 868  800 + 60 + 8  seven hundred seventy-three  700 + 70 + 3

11. 765 _____ + _____ + _____
12. 557 _____ + _____ + _____
13. 186 _____ + _____ + _____
14. 914 _____ + _____ + _____
15. 215 _____ + _____ + _____

16. four hundred forty-five  _____ + _____ + _____
17. two hundred fourteen  _____ + _____ + _____
18. one hundred fifty-one  _____ + _____ + _____
19. three hundred eighty-one _____ + _____ + _____
20. six hundred twenty-three _____ + _____ + _____

Write the following using only words.

**Example:** 418  four hundred eighteen

21. 129 _____

22. 365 _____

23. 790 _____

24. 661 _____

25. 296 _____

# Practice 24

Counting by ones write the number that comes before each problem.

| | | | |
|---|---|---|---|
| **1.** 350 _____ | **6.** 810 _____ | **11.** 295 _____ | **16.** 784 _____ |
| **2.** 678 _____ | **7.** 577 _____ | **12.** 473 _____ | **17.** 264 _____ |
| **3.** 209 _____ | **8.** 548 _____ | **13.** 317 _____ | **18.** 218 _____ |
| **4.** 151 _____ | **9.** 314 _____ | **14.** 376 _____ | **19.** 832 _____ |
| **5.** 568 _____ | **10.** 231 _____ | **15.** 908 _____ | **20.** 211 _____ |

Write the number that comes in between.

Write the number that comes after.

| | | |
|---|---|---|
| **21.** 895 _____ 897 | **31.** 164 _____ 166 | **41.** 389 _____ |
| **22.** 115 _____ 117 | **32.** 334 _____ 336 | **42.** 278 _____ |
| **23.** 162 _____ 164 | **33.** 306 _____ 308 | **43.** 342 _____ |
| **24.** 847 _____ 849 | **34.** 439 _____ 441 | **44.** 644 _____ |
| **25.** 873 _____ 875 | **35.** 125 _____ 127 | **45.** 713 _____ |
| **26.** 107 _____ 109 | **36.** 626 _____ 628 | **46.** 107 _____ |
| **27.** 722 _____ 724 | **37.** 807 _____ 809 | **47.** 638 _____ |
| **28.** 119 _____ 121 | **38.** 436 _____ 438 | **48.** 260 _____ |
| **29.** 426 _____ 428 | **39.** 258 _____ 260 | **49.** 369 _____ |
| **30.** 277 _____ 279 | **40.** 541 _____ 543 | **50.** 785 _____ |

# Practice 25

Solve each problem.

1.　528
　　+ 261

2.　341
　　+ 528

3.　376
　　+ 401

4.　513
　　+ 123

5.　117
　　+ 760

6.　192
　　+ 604

7.　349
　　+ 640

8.　229
　　+ 110

9.　425
　　+ 362

10.　431
　　+ 135

11.　174
　　+ 721

12.　306
　　+ 481

13.　872
　　+ 114

14.　588
　　+ 311

15.　575
　　+ 203

16.　312
　　+ 156

17.　199
　　+ 400

18.　335
　　+ 244

19.　385
　　+ 614

20.　860
　　+ 127

# **Practice 26** ⤿ ⬳ ⤿ ⬳ ⤿ ⬳ ⤿ ⬳ ⤿ ⬳ ⤿ ⬳ ⤿ ⬳ ⬳

Solve each problem.

1.  $ 103
   + $  96

2.  $ 157
   + $ 612

3.  $ 180
   + $ 319

4.  $ 138
   + $ 641

5.  $ 238
   + $ 440

6.  $ 254
   + $ 734

7.  $ 876
   + $ 100

8.  $ 517
   + $ 180

9.  $ 192
   + $ 106

10. $ 512
   + $ 305

11. $ 406
   + $ 323

12. $ 374
   + $ 222

13. $ 438
   + $ 520

14. $ 727
   + $ 271

15. $ 202
   + $ 644

16. $ 450
   + $ 208

17. $ 364
   + $ 133

18. $ 152
   + $ 817

19. $ 891
   + $ 103

20. $ 381
   + $ 406

# **Practice 27**

Solve each problem.

1.  729
    + 137

2.  789
    + 103

3.  573
    + 241

4.  210
    + 693

5.  165
    + 162

6.  356
    + 406

7.  546
    + 445

8.  268
    + 712

9.  576
    + 381

10. 406
    + 460

11. 253
    + 576

12. 241
    + 274

13. 508
    + 259

14. 194
    + 111

15. 104
    + 187

16. 652
    + 253

17. 353
    + 253

18. 829
    + 111

19. 835
    + 125

20. 877
    + 103

# Practice 28 ꙮ ꙮ ꙮ ꙮ ꙮ ꙮ ꙮ ꙮ ꙮ ꙮ ꙮ ꙮ ꙮ

Find the total amount of each bank deposit.

1. Amy made two deposits this week, one deposit for $380 and one for $300. How much did Amy deposit in all? _____.

2. Chad deposited two checks from his Aunt and Uncle. One check was for $516 and the other check was for $172. How much did Chad deposit in all?

   _____.

3. Carrie deposited a $100 refund check and her paycheck in the amount of $559. How much did Carrie deposit in all? _____.

4. Lon deposited a rebate check in the amount of $612 and a birthday check in the amount of $100. How much did Lon deposit in all? _____.

5. Jeremy sold 862 matches and 128 candles. How many items in all did Jeremy sell? _____.

6. Janet sold 804 flashlights and 108 packs of batteries. How many items did Janet sell in all? _____.

7. Annette sold 677 pairs of mittens and 214 pairs of gloves. How many items did Annette sell in all? _____.

8. Ryan sold 385 pairs of long johns and 508 pairs of thick socks. How many items did Ryan sell in all? _____.

9. Kelly sold 444 ski jackets and 436 pairs of ski pants. How many items did Kelly sell in all? _____.

10. John sold 437 caps and 119 hats. How many items did John sell in all?

    _____.

# Practice 29

Solve each problem.

| | | | | |
|---|---|---|---|---|
| **1.** 744<br>− 732 | **2.** 367<br>− 130 | **3.** 899<br>− 459 | **4.** 215<br>− 113 | **5.** 642<br>− 602 |
| **6.** 980<br>− 950 | **7.** 691<br>− 540 | **8.** 288<br>− 231 | **9.** 686<br>− 525 | **10.** 849<br>− 537 |
| **11.** 258<br>− 100 | **12.** 917<br>− 714 | **13.** 367<br>− 364 | **14.** 891<br>− 171 | **15.** 339<br>− 216 |
| **16.** 484<br>− 373 | **17.** 648<br>− 346 | **18.** 776<br>− 550 | **19.** 664<br>− 542 | **20.** 893<br>− 312 |

# Practice 30

Solve each problem. Write the letter that goes with each difference on the line.

| **A** | **B** | **C** | **D** | **E** |
|---|---|---|---|---|
| 1. 267<br>– 117 | 2. 974<br>– 543 | 3. 479<br>– 339 | 4. 897<br>– 427 | 5. 955<br>– 651 |

| **F** | **H** | **I** | **L** | **M** |
|---|---|---|---|---|
| 6. 973<br>– 361 | 7. 289<br>– 126 | 8. 381<br>– 141 | 9. 515<br>– 314 | 10. 254<br>– 131 |

| **N** | **O** | **P** | **R** | **S** |
|---|---|---|---|---|
| 11. 425<br>– 325 | 12. 916<br>– 713 | 13. 525<br>– 122 | 14. 826<br>– 804 | 15. 886<br>– 153 |

| **T** | **U** | **V** | **W** | **Z** |
|---|---|---|---|---|
| 16. 766<br>– 664 | 17. 884<br>– 881 | 17. 469<br>– 119 | 18. 826<br>– 125 | 20. 917<br>– 417 |

$$\overline{\phantom{xx}}_{240}\quad \overline{\phantom{xx}}_{140}\ \overline{\phantom{xx}}_{150}\ \overline{\phantom{xx}}_{100}\qquad \overline{\phantom{xx}}_{733}\ \overline{\phantom{xx}}_{3}\ \overline{\phantom{xx}}_{431}\ \overline{\phantom{xx}}_{102}\ \overline{\phantom{xx}}_{22}\ \overline{\phantom{xx}}_{150}\ \overline{\phantom{xx}}_{140}\ \overline{\phantom{xx}}_{102}$$

$$\overline{\phantom{xx}}_{240}\ \overline{\phantom{xx}}_{100}\qquad \overline{\phantom{xx}}_{150}\qquad \overline{\phantom{xx}}_{612}\ \overline{\phantom{xx}}_{201}\ \overline{\phantom{xx}}_{150}\ \overline{\phantom{xx}}_{733}\ \overline{\phantom{xx}}_{163}\ !$$

# **Practice 31**

Solve each problem.

| | | | | |
|---|---|---|---|---|
| **1.** $805$ $-\ 471$ | **2.** $304$ $-\ 184$ | **3.** $223$ $-\ 216$ | **4.** $984$ $-\ 439$ | **5.** $481$ $-\ 129$ |
| **6.** $805$ $-\ 471$ | **7.** $882$ $-\ 575$ | **8.** $566$ $-\ 257$ | **9.** $531$ $-\ 526$ | **10.** $819$ $-\ 774$ |
| **11.** $713$ $-\ 306$ | **12.** $603$ $-\ 180$ | **13.** $993$ $-\ 745$ | **14.** $992$ $-\ 166$ | **15.** $921$ $-\ 814$ |
| **16.** $611$ $-\ 370$ | **17.** $784$ $-\ 594$ | **18.** $956$ $-\ 737$ | **19.** $624$ $-\ 543$ | **20.** $754$ $-\ 162$ |

# Practice 32

Solve the problems below and write the answers in the puzzle.

**Down**

1.  689
   − 599

2.  583
   − 436

4.  681
   − 419

5.  886
   − 437

6.  768
   − 285

8.  529
   − 446

10. 802
   − 141

11. 963
   − 507

12. 796
   − 747

14. 786
   − 518

15. 723
   − 453

16. 737
   − 192

**Across**

2.  700
   − 570

3.  941
   − 214

6.  694
   − 265

7.  928
   − 230

9.  828
   − 792

11. 607
   − 173

13. 861
   − 735

15. 573
   − 293

17. 607
   − 127

# Practice 33

Count by 5s and 10s to solve these problems.

**1.**  _____¢

**2.**  _____¢

**3.**

_____¢ or $_____

**4.**

_____¢ or $_____

**5.**

_____¢ or $_____

**6.**

_____¢ or $_____

**7.**

_____¢ or $_____

**8.**

_____¢ or $_____

**9.**

_____¢ or $_____

**10.**

_____¢ or $_____

**11.**

_____¢ or $_____

# Practice 34

Count by 25s.

**1.**

_____¢

**2.**

_____¢

**3.**

$_____

**4.**

$_____

Write the amount two ways.

**5.**

_____¢ or $_____

**6.**

_____¢ or $_____

**7.**

_____¢ or $_____

**8.**

_____¢ or $_____

**9.**

_____¢ or $_____

**10.**

_____¢ or $_____

**11.**

_____¢ or $_____

**12.**

_____¢ or $_____

**13.**
_____¢ or $_____

*Fractions*

# Practice 35

Write the number of equal parts.

1.    2.    3.    4.    5.

_____   _____   _____   _____   _____

6.    7.    8.    9.    10.

_____   _____   _____   _____   _____

Write the number of shaded parts.

11.    12.    13.    14.    15.

_____   _____   _____   _____   _____

16.    17.    18.    19.    20.

_____   _____   _____   _____   _____

Write the fraction.
- The top number is the numerator.  It tells how many parts are shaded.
- The bottom number is the denominator.  It tells how many parts in all.

21.    22.    23.    24.    25.

_____   _____   _____   _____   _____

26.    27.    28.    29.    30.

_____   _____   _____   _____   _____

*#8602 Practice Makes Perfect: Place Value*     *© Teacher Created Resources, Inc.*

# Practice 36

Name the fraction that is shaded.

1.
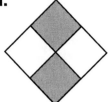
_____

2.
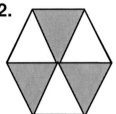
_____

3.
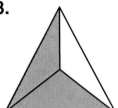
_____

4.
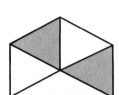
_____

5.
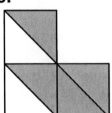
_____

6.
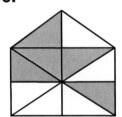
_____

7.
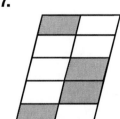
_____

8.
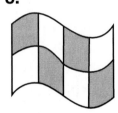
_____

9.
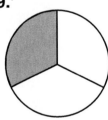
_____

10.
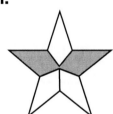
_____

11.
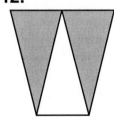
_____

12.
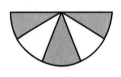
_____

13.
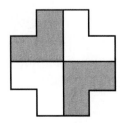
_____

14.
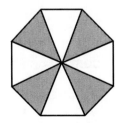
_____

15.

_____

16.

_____

# Test Practice 1

Fill in the circle for the correct answer.

**1.** Which one shows 4?

    Ⓐ    Ⓑ    Ⓒ

**2.** Which one shows 2?

    Ⓐ    Ⓑ    Ⓒ

**3.** Which one shows 10?

    Ⓐ    Ⓑ    Ⓒ

**4.** Which one is more?

| 7 | 5 | 3 |
|---|---|---|
| Ⓐ | Ⓑ | Ⓒ |

**5.** Which one is more?

| 11 | 23 | 15 |
|----|----|----|
| Ⓐ | Ⓑ | Ⓒ |

**6.** Which one is more?

| 8 | 7 | 5 |
|---|---|---|
| Ⓐ | Ⓑ | Ⓒ |

**7.** Which one is less?

| 9 | 2 | 1 |
|---|---|---|
| Ⓐ | Ⓑ | Ⓒ |

**8.** Which one is less?

| 17 | 16 | 15 |
|----|----|----|
| Ⓐ | Ⓑ | Ⓒ |

**9.** Which one is less?

| 4 | 18 | 12 |
|---|----|----|
| Ⓐ | Ⓑ | Ⓒ |

**10.** Choose the number word.

**ten**

| 10 | 12 | 2 |
|----|----|---|
| Ⓐ | Ⓑ | Ⓒ |

**11.** Choose the number word.

**eight**

| 1 | 7 | 8 |
|---|---|---|
| Ⓐ | Ⓑ | Ⓒ |

**12.** Choose the number word.

**four**

| 5 | 4 | 3 |
|---|---|---|
| Ⓐ | Ⓑ | Ⓒ |

**13.** What number comes before 6?

| 7 | 5 | 8 |
|---|---|---|
| Ⓐ | Ⓑ | Ⓒ |

**14.** Which number comes after 3?

| 2 | 4 | 1 |
|---|---|---|
| Ⓐ | Ⓑ | Ⓒ |

**15.** Which number comes in between 7 and 9?

| 10 | 6 | 8 |
|----|---|---|
| Ⓐ | Ⓑ | Ⓒ |

# Test Practice 2

Fill in the circle under the correct answer.

**1.** How many tens?

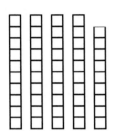

| 9 | 4 | 49 |
|---|---|----|
| Ⓐ | Ⓑ | Ⓒ |

**2.** How many ones?

| 2 | 27 | 7 |
|---|----|---|
| Ⓐ | Ⓑ | Ⓒ |

**3.** Name the number.

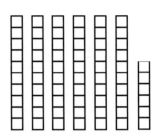

| 56 | 66 | 65 |
|----|----|----|
| Ⓐ | Ⓑ | Ⓒ |

**4.** Name the number.

fourteen

| 14 | 41 | 5 |
|----|----|---|
| Ⓐ | Ⓑ | Ⓒ |

**5.** Compare the numbers.

12 ◯ 15

| > | < | = |
|---|---|---|
| Ⓐ | Ⓑ | Ⓒ |

**6.** Compare the numbers.

18 ◯ 52

| > | < | = |
|---|---|---|
| Ⓐ | Ⓑ | Ⓒ |

**7.** Read the number word.

**eighteen**

| 8 | 18 | 89 |
|---|----|----|
| Ⓐ | Ⓑ | Ⓒ |

**8.** Read the number word.

**thirty-one**

| 30 | 13 | 31 |
|----|----|----|
| Ⓐ | Ⓑ | Ⓒ |

**9.** Write in standard form.

**40 + 7**

| 47 | 407 | 470 |
|----|-----|-----|
| Ⓐ | Ⓑ | Ⓒ |

**10.** Write in standard form.

**20 + 6**

| 26 | 206 | 260 |
|----|-----|-----|
| Ⓐ | Ⓑ | Ⓒ |

**11.** Write in standard form.

**three tens + seven ones**

| 307 | 30 | 37 |
|-----|----|----|
| Ⓐ | Ⓑ | Ⓒ |

**12.** Write in standard form.

**5 tens + 9 ones**

| 59 | 50 | 95 |
|----|----|----|
| Ⓐ | Ⓑ | Ⓒ |

**13.** Add.

**34 + 24**

| 13 | 69 | 58 |
|----|----|----|
| Ⓐ | Ⓑ | Ⓒ |

**14.** Add.

**62 + 30**

| 92 | 32 | 65 |
|----|----|----|
| Ⓐ | Ⓑ | Ⓒ |

**15.** Add.

**28 + 51**

| 38 | 23 | 79 |
|----|----|----|
| Ⓐ | Ⓑ | Ⓒ |

# Test Practice 3

Fill in the circle for the correct answer.

**1.** Add.

$$15$$
$$+ \ 29$$

44    34    39
Ⓐ    Ⓑ    Ⓒ

**2.** Add.

$$37$$
$$+ \ 19$$

416    46    56
Ⓐ    Ⓑ    Ⓒ

**3.** Add.

$$47$$
$$+ \ 44$$

91    81    87
Ⓐ    Ⓑ    Ⓒ

**4.** Add.

$$39$$
$$+ \ 42$$

81    71    91
Ⓐ    Ⓑ    Ⓒ

**5.** Add.

$$16$$
$$+ \ 68$$

56    67    84
Ⓐ    Ⓑ    Ⓒ

**6.** Add.

$$60$$
$$+ \ 32$$

96    77    92
Ⓐ    Ⓑ    Ⓒ

**7.** Subtract.

$$53 - 51$$

3    2    1
Ⓐ    Ⓑ    Ⓒ

**8.** Subtract.

$$37 - 10$$

27    17    7
Ⓐ    Ⓑ    Ⓒ

**9.** Subtract.

$$72 - 21$$

71    51    50
Ⓐ    Ⓑ    Ⓒ

**10.** Subtract.

$$61 - 46$$

15    25    17
Ⓐ    Ⓑ    Ⓒ

**11.** Subtract.

$$91 - 49$$

140    52    42
Ⓐ    Ⓑ    Ⓒ

**12.** Subtract.

$$41 - 36$$

5    15    17
Ⓐ    Ⓑ    Ⓒ

**13.** Complete the table.

|     | – 8 |
| --- | --- |
| 15  | 7   |
| 79  | ?   |

78    71    87
Ⓐ    Ⓑ    Ⓒ

**14.** Complete the table.

|     | – 5 |
| --- | --- |
| 76  | ?   |
| 14  | 9   |

81    85    71
Ⓐ    Ⓑ    Ⓒ

**15.** Complete the table.

|     | – 4 |
| --- | --- |
| 31  | ?   |
| 46  | 42  |

34    35    27
Ⓐ    Ⓑ    Ⓒ

# Test Practice 4

Fill in the circle for the correct answer.

**1.** Name the number.

**four hundred forty-six**

446    4046    464
Ⓐ     Ⓑ     Ⓒ

**2.** Name the number.

**five hundred twenty-two**

520    225    522
Ⓐ     Ⓑ     Ⓒ

**3.** Name the number.

**700 + 50 + 3**

7053    753    70053
Ⓐ     Ⓑ     Ⓒ

**4.** Name the number.

**900 + 1**

901    91    9001
Ⓐ     Ⓑ     Ⓒ

**5.** Name the number.

**7 hundreds + 6 ones**

76    706    7006
Ⓐ     Ⓑ     Ⓒ

**6.** Name the number.

**8 hundreds + 7 tens + 1 one**

801    781    871
Ⓐ     Ⓑ     Ⓒ

**7.** How many hundreds?

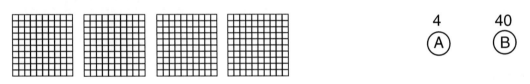

4    40    400
Ⓐ    Ⓑ    Ⓒ

**8.** Write the number.

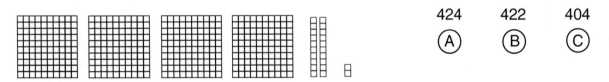

424    422    404
Ⓐ    Ⓑ    Ⓒ

**9.** Name the place value of the underlined digit.
**5̲69**

ones   tens   hundreds
Ⓐ     Ⓑ     Ⓒ

**10.** Name the place value of the largest digit.
**449̲**

ones   tens   hundreds
Ⓐ     Ⓑ     Ⓒ

**11.** Which number is smallest?

65    46    15
Ⓐ    Ⓑ    Ⓒ

**12.** Compare the numbers.

681_____232

>    <    =
Ⓐ    Ⓑ    Ⓒ

**13.** Compare the numbers.

915_____431

>    <    =
Ⓐ    Ⓑ    Ⓒ

**14.** Compare the numbers.

114_____703

>    <    =
Ⓐ    Ⓑ    Ⓒ

# Test Practice 5

Fill in the circle for the correct answer.

**1.** Add.

$$300 + 600$$

| 360 | 900 | 630 |
|-----|-----|-----|
| Ⓐ | Ⓑ | Ⓒ |

**2.** Add.

$$200 + 300$$

| 500 | 230 | 3000 |
|-----|-----|------|
| Ⓐ | Ⓑ | Ⓒ |

**3.** Add.

$$700 + 400$$

| 1,100 | 300 | 400 |
|-------|-----|-----|
| Ⓐ | Ⓑ | Ⓒ |

**4.** Compare the numbers.

$$200 + 100 \bigcirc 600$$

| > | < | = |
|---|---|---|
| Ⓐ | Ⓑ | Ⓒ |

**5.** Compare the numbers.

$$700 + 300 \bigcirc 600$$

| > | < | = |
|---|---|---|
| Ⓐ | Ⓑ | Ⓒ |

**6.** Compare the numbers.

$$800 + 800 \bigcirc 700$$

| > | < | = |
|---|---|---|
| Ⓐ | Ⓑ | Ⓒ |

**7.** Which number comes before **283**?

| 282 | 284 | 285 |
|-----|-----|-----|
| Ⓐ | Ⓑ | Ⓒ |

**8.** Which number comes before **359**?

| 360 | 357 | 358 |
|-----|-----|-----|
| Ⓐ | Ⓑ | Ⓒ |

**9.** Which number comes after **377**?

| 380 | 378 | 376 |
|-----|-----|-----|
| Ⓐ | Ⓑ | Ⓒ |

**10.** Which number comes after **448**?

| 447 | 449 | 450 |
|-----|-----|-----|
| Ⓐ | Ⓑ | Ⓒ |

**11.** Which number comes in between **842** and **844**?

| 843 | 841 | 845 |
|-----|-----|-----|
| Ⓐ | Ⓑ | Ⓒ |

**12.** Which number comes in between **796** and **798**?

| 795 | 797 | 799 |
|-----|-----|-----|
| Ⓐ | Ⓑ | Ⓒ |

**13.** Numbers to use: 1, 2, 3. I am an even number. The 1 is in the tens place. What number am I?

| 213 | 312 | 123 |
|-----|-----|-----|
| Ⓐ | Ⓑ | Ⓒ |

**14.** Numbers to use: 1, 9, 9. Both of the 9's are next to each other. The 1 is in the ones place. What number am I?

| 991 | 199 | 919 |
|-----|-----|-----|
| Ⓐ | Ⓑ | Ⓒ |

**15.** Numbers to use: 1, 4, 7. I am an odd number. The 4 is in the tens place. The 1 has the greatest value. What number am I?

| 741 | 471 | 147 |
|-----|-----|-----|
| Ⓐ | Ⓑ | Ⓒ |

# Test Practice 6

Fill in the circle under the correct answer.

**1.** Add.

$$\begin{array}{r} 518 \\ + 150 \\ \hline \end{array}$$

| 684 | 686 | 668 |
|:---:|:---:|:---:|
| Ⓐ | Ⓑ | Ⓒ |

**2.** Add.

$$\begin{array}{r} \$169 \\ + \$110 \\ \hline \end{array}$$

| $279 | $289 | $297 |
|:---:|:---:|:---:|
| Ⓐ | Ⓑ | Ⓒ |

**3.** Subtract.

$$\begin{array}{r} 520 \\ - 110 \\ \hline \end{array}$$

| 630 | 410 | 430 |
|:---:|:---:|:---:|
| Ⓐ | Ⓑ | Ⓒ |

**4.** Subtract.

$$\begin{array}{r} 353 \\ - 201 \\ \hline \end{array}$$

| 154 | 554 | 152 |
|:---:|:---:|:---:|
| Ⓐ | Ⓑ | Ⓒ |

**5.** Add.

$$\begin{array}{r} 668 \\ + 126 \\ \hline \end{array}$$

| 874 | 784 | 794 |
|:---:|:---:|:---:|
| Ⓐ | Ⓑ | Ⓒ |

**6.** Add.

$$\begin{array}{r} 457 \\ + 537 \\ \hline \end{array}$$

| 987 | 1,094 | 994 |
|:---:|:---:|:---:|
| Ⓐ | Ⓑ | Ⓒ |

**7.** Subtract.

$$\begin{array}{r} 661 \\ - 201 \\ \hline \end{array}$$

| 560 | 360 | 460 |
|:---:|:---:|:---:|
| Ⓐ | Ⓑ | Ⓒ |

**8.** Subtract.

$$\begin{array}{r} 198 \\ - 126 \\ \hline \end{array}$$

| 72 | 84 | 62 |
|:---:|:---:|:---:|
| Ⓐ | Ⓑ | Ⓒ |

**9.** Subtract.

$$\begin{array}{r} 296 \\ - 168 \\ \hline \end{array}$$

| 125 | 128 | 138 |
|:---:|:---:|:---:|
| Ⓐ | Ⓑ | Ⓒ |

**10.** Count by 25.

**25,_____, 75, 100**

| 30 | 50 | 40 |
|:---:|:---:|:---:|
| Ⓐ | Ⓑ | Ⓒ |

**11.** Count by 25.

**325, 350,_____, 400**

| 375 | 365 | 425 |
|:---:|:---:|:---:|
| Ⓐ | Ⓑ | Ⓒ |

**12.** Count by 50.

**800,_____, 900, 950**

| 850 | 875 | 925 |
|:---:|:---:|:---:|
| Ⓐ | Ⓑ | Ⓒ |

# Answer Sheet

## Test Practice 1

1. Ⓐ Ⓑ Ⓒ    4. Ⓐ Ⓑ Ⓒ    7. Ⓐ Ⓑ Ⓒ    10. Ⓐ Ⓑ Ⓒ    13. Ⓐ Ⓑ Ⓒ

2. Ⓐ Ⓑ Ⓒ    5. Ⓐ Ⓑ Ⓒ    8. Ⓐ Ⓑ Ⓒ    11. Ⓐ Ⓑ Ⓒ    14. Ⓐ Ⓑ Ⓒ

3. Ⓐ Ⓑ Ⓒ    6. Ⓐ Ⓑ Ⓒ    9. Ⓐ Ⓑ Ⓒ    12. Ⓐ Ⓑ Ⓒ    15. Ⓐ Ⓑ Ⓒ

## Test Practice 2

1. Ⓐ Ⓑ Ⓒ    4. Ⓐ Ⓑ Ⓒ    7. Ⓐ Ⓑ Ⓒ    10. Ⓐ Ⓑ Ⓒ    13. Ⓐ Ⓑ Ⓒ

2. Ⓐ Ⓑ Ⓒ    5. Ⓐ Ⓑ Ⓒ    8. Ⓐ Ⓑ Ⓒ    11. Ⓐ Ⓑ Ⓒ    14. Ⓐ Ⓑ Ⓒ

3. Ⓐ Ⓑ Ⓒ    6. Ⓐ Ⓑ Ⓒ    9. Ⓐ Ⓑ Ⓒ    12. Ⓐ Ⓑ Ⓒ    15. Ⓐ Ⓑ Ⓒ

## Test Practice 3

1. Ⓐ Ⓑ Ⓒ    4. Ⓐ Ⓑ Ⓒ    7. Ⓐ Ⓑ Ⓒ    10. Ⓐ Ⓑ Ⓒ    13. Ⓐ Ⓑ Ⓒ

2. Ⓐ Ⓑ Ⓒ    5. Ⓐ Ⓑ Ⓒ    8. Ⓐ Ⓑ Ⓒ    11. Ⓐ Ⓑ Ⓒ    14. Ⓐ Ⓑ Ⓒ

3. Ⓐ Ⓑ Ⓒ    6. Ⓐ Ⓑ Ⓒ    9. Ⓐ Ⓑ Ⓒ    12. Ⓐ Ⓑ Ⓒ    15. Ⓐ Ⓑ Ⓒ

## Test Practice 4

1. Ⓐ Ⓑ Ⓒ    4. Ⓐ Ⓑ Ⓒ    7. Ⓐ Ⓑ Ⓒ    10. Ⓐ Ⓑ Ⓒ    13. Ⓐ Ⓑ Ⓒ

2. Ⓐ Ⓑ Ⓒ    5. Ⓐ Ⓑ Ⓒ    8. Ⓐ Ⓑ Ⓒ    11. Ⓐ Ⓑ Ⓒ    14. Ⓐ Ⓑ Ⓒ

3. Ⓐ Ⓑ Ⓒ    6. Ⓐ Ⓑ Ⓒ    9. Ⓐ Ⓑ Ⓒ    12. Ⓐ Ⓑ Ⓒ

## Test Practice 5

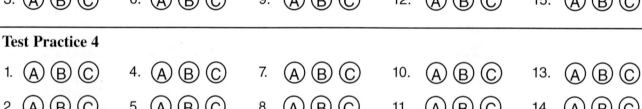

1. Ⓐ Ⓑ Ⓒ    4. Ⓐ Ⓑ Ⓒ    7. Ⓐ Ⓑ Ⓒ    10. Ⓐ Ⓑ Ⓒ    13. Ⓐ Ⓑ Ⓒ

2. Ⓐ Ⓑ Ⓒ    5. Ⓐ Ⓑ Ⓒ    8. Ⓐ Ⓑ Ⓒ    11. Ⓐ Ⓑ Ⓒ    14. Ⓐ Ⓑ Ⓒ

3. Ⓐ Ⓑ Ⓒ    6. Ⓐ Ⓑ Ⓒ    9. Ⓐ Ⓑ Ⓒ    12. Ⓐ Ⓑ Ⓒ    15. Ⓐ Ⓑ Ⓒ

## Test Practice 6

1. Ⓐ Ⓑ Ⓒ    4. Ⓐ Ⓑ Ⓒ    7. Ⓐ Ⓑ Ⓒ    10. Ⓐ Ⓑ Ⓒ

2. Ⓐ Ⓑ Ⓒ    5. Ⓐ Ⓑ Ⓒ    8. Ⓐ Ⓑ Ⓒ    11. Ⓐ Ⓑ Ⓒ

3. Ⓐ Ⓑ Ⓒ    6. Ⓐ Ⓑ Ⓒ    9. Ⓐ Ⓑ Ⓒ    12. Ⓐ Ⓑ Ⓒ

# Answer Key

## Page 4
1. 5 blocks
2. 3 blocks
3. 9 blocks
4. 0 blocks
5. 7 blocks
6. 4 blocks
7. 1 block
8. 6 blocks
9. 8 blocks
10. 2 blocks
11. 8
12. 5
13. 5
14. 10
15. 4
16. 7
17. 9
18. 2
19. 8
20. 6
21. 5
22. 7
23. 9
24. 2
25. 6
26. 2
27. 4
28. 3
29. 0
30. 3
31. 0
32. 1
33. 3
34. 5

## Page 5
1. 1 ten, 8 ones
2. 1 ten, 6 ones
3. 2 tens, 8 ones
4. 2 tens, 4 ones
5. 1 ten, 0 ones
6. 1 ten, 4 ones
7. 1 ten, 9 ones
8. 0 tens, 8 ones

## Page 6
1. 2 tens = 20
2. 5 tens = 50
3. 4 tens = 40
4. 8 tens = 80
5. 1 ten = 10
6. 3 tens = 30
7. 7 tens = 70
8. 6 tens = 60
9. 11
10. 12
11. 13
12. 14
13. 15
14. 16
15. 17
16. 18
17. 19
18. 20
19. 25
20. 30
21. 40
22. 50
23. 60
24. 70
25. 75
26. 80
27. 90
28. 100

## Page 7
1. 27
2. 2
3. 19
4. 15
5. 43
6. 8
7. 32
8. 44
9. 26
10. 31
11. 10

## Page 8
1. 64
2. 76
3. 83
4. 90
5. 68
6. 82
7. 74
8. 75
9. 97
10. 51
11. 57

## Page 9
1. <
2. >
3. <
4. >
5. <
6. <
7. >
8. <
9. >
10. >
11. <
12. <

## Page 10
1. 23
2. 14
3. 39
4. 37
5. 69
6. 98
7. 44
8. 53
9. 70
10. 81
11. 85
12. 10
13. 17
14. 94
15. 41
16. 20 + 8
17. 10 + 6
18. 60 + 1
19. 80 + 3
20. 40 + 0
21. 70 + 3
22. 10 + 5
23. 30 + 0
24. 80 + 2
25. 50 + 5
26. twenty-two
27. fifty-six
28. ninety-two
29. forty-six
30. thirty-seven
31. eighty-one
32. forty-four
33. sixty-eight
34. thirty-five
35. ten

## Page 11
1. 91
2. 67
3. 88
4. 20
5. 54
6. 34
7. 69
8. 89
9. 49
10. 93
11. 69
12. 78
13. 56
14. 34
15. 35
16. 94
17. 89
18. 65
19. 68
20. 96

## Page 12
1. 67
2. 84
3. 87
4. 98
5. 65
6. 87
7. 66
8. 78
9. 78
10. 32
11. 79
12. 96
13. 77
14. 77
15. 56
16. 65
17. 99
18. 65
19. 89
20. 89

## Page 13
1. 93
2. 93
3. 70
4. 92
5. 34
6. 80
7. 81
8. 95
9. 70
10. 82
11. 71
12. 62

## Page 14
1. 90
2. 91
3. 81
4. 92
5. 91
6. 73
7. 95
8. 94
9. 63
10. 94
11. 93
12. 91
13. 55
14. 94
15. 93
16. 72
17. 84
18. 91
19. 42
20. 81

## Page 15
1. 8 + 12 = 20
2. 17 + 16 = 33
3. 18 + 24 = 42
4. 25 + 28 = 53
5. 13 + 19 = 32
6. 37 + 45 = 82
7. 34 + 47 = 81
8. 12 + 39 = 51
9. 17 + 29 = 46
10. 39 + 24 = 63

## Page 16
1. 19 + 16 = 35 miles
2. 19 + 37 = 56 miles
3. 45 + 19 = 64 miles
4. 26 + 14 = 40 miles
5. 37 + 26 = 63 miles
6. 45 + 16 = 61 miles
7. 45 + 24 = 69 miles
8. 26 + 18 = 44 miles
9. 18 + 24 = 42 miles
10. <
11. <
12. <
13. <

## Page 17
1. 36
2. 66
3. 37
4. 56
5. 33
6. 47
7. 5
8. 2
9. 36
10. 61
11. 41
12. 60
13. 0
14. 50
15. 62
16. 91, 30, 61, 83, 42, 16
17. 83, 72, 25, 41, 13, 51
18. 21, 90, 10, 13, 85, 30

## Page 18
1. 36
2. 66
3. 37
4. 56
5. 33
6. 47
7. 5
8. 2
9. 36
10. 61
11. 41
12. 60
13. 96¢ – 60¢ = 36¢
14. 88¢ – 77¢ = 11¢
15. 94¢ – 21¢ = 73¢
16. 53¢ – 11¢ = 42¢
17. 86¢ – 31¢ = 55¢
18. 57¢ – 17¢ = 40¢

## Page 19
1. 49
2. 9
3. 19
4. 65
5. 63
6. 18
7. 35
8. 18
9. 7
10. 44
11. 57
12. 54
13. 18
14. 38
15. 26
16. 27
17. 73
18. 17
19. 16
20. 57

## Page 20
1. 36; 36 + 47 = 83
2. 21; 21 + 59 = 80
3. 19; 19 + 31 = 50
4. 37; 37 + 19 = 56
5. 19; 19 + 13 = 32
6. 27; 27 + 67 = 94
7. 9; 9 + 79 = 88
8. 7; 56 + 7 = 63
9. 27; 27 + 33 = 60
10. 24; 24 + 17 = 41
11. 26; 26 + 69 = 95
12. 36; 36 + 27 = 63
13. 37; 37 + 44 = 81
14. 9; 9 + 16 = 25
15. 15; 15 + 75 = 90

## Page 21
1. 600
2. 800
3. 400
4. 300
5. 100
6. 500
7. 200
8. 700

## Page 22
1. 5 hundreds + 1 ten + 2 ones; 500 + 10 + 2; 512
2. 2 hundreds + 1 ten + 9 ones; 200 + 10 + 9; 219
3. 3 hundreds + 8 tens + 6 ones; 300 + 80 + 6; 386
4. 7 hundreds + 1 ten + 0 ones; 700 + 10 + 0; 710
5. 4 hundreds + 5 tens + 7 ones; 400 + 50 + 7; 457
6. 9 hundreds + 0 tens + 3 ones; 900 + 0 + 3; 903

## Page 23
1. 4 hundreds + 4 tens + 4 ones; 400 + 40 + 4; 444
2. 1 hundred + 9 tens + 2 ones; 100 + 90 + 2; 192
3. 6 hundreds + 7 tens + 6 ones; 600 + 70 + 6; 676
4. 3 hundreds + 4 tens + 6 ones; 300 + 40 + 6; 346
5. 1 hundred + 6 tens + 8 ones; 100 + 60 + 8; 168
6. 4 hundreds + 1 ten + 8 ones; 400 + 10 + 8; 418

## Page 24
1. ones
2. tens
3. ones
4. ones
5. hundreds
6. ones
7. 8, hundreds
8. 8, ones
9. 6, tens
10. 9, hundreds
11. 9, tens
12. 9, hundreds
13. 944, hundreds
14. 375, tens
15. 932, hundreds
16. 851, hundreds
17. 677, ones
18. 199, tens

## Page 25
1. 400
2. 900
3. 100
4. 200
5. 300
6. 0
7. 400
8. 600
9. 200
10. 100
11. 200
12. 400
13. =
14. <
15. >
16. =
17. >
18. =
19. >
20. >
21. >
22. =
23. <
24. >

# Answer Key (cont.)

## Page 26
1. 778
2. 406
3. 233
4. 491
5. 247
6. 396
7. 564
8. 125
9. 987
10. 699
11. 700 + 60 + 5
12. 500 + 50 + 7
13. 100 + 80 + 6
14. 900 + 10 + 4
15. 200 + 10 + 5
16. 400 + 40 + 5
17. 200 + 10 + 4
18. 100 + 50 + 1
19. 300 + 80 + 1
20. 600 + 20 + 3
21. one hundred twenty-nine
22. three hundred sixty-five
23. seven hundred ninety
24. six hundred sixty-one
25. two hundred ninety-six

## Page 27
1. 349
2. 677
3. 208
4. 150
5. 567
6. 809
7. 576
8. 547
9. 313
10. 230
11. 294
12. 472
13. 316
14. 375
15. 907
16. 783
17. 263
18. 217
19. 831
20. 210
21. 896
22. 116
23. 163
24. 848
25. 874
26. 108
27. 723
28. 120
29. 427
30. 278
31. 165
32. 335
33. 307
34. 440
35. 126
36. 627
37. 808
38. 437
39. 259
40. 542
41. 390
42. 279
43. 343
44. 645
45. 714
46. 108
47. 639
48. 261
49. 370
50. 786

## Page 28
1. 789
2. 869
3. 777
4. 636
5. 877
6. 796
7. 989
8. 339
9. 787
10. 566
11. 895
12. 787
13. 986
14. 899
15. 778
16. 468
17. 599
18. 579
19. 999
20. 987

## Page 29
1. $199
2. $769
3. $499
4. $779
5. $678
6. $988
7. $976
8. $697
9. $298
10. $817
11. $729
12. $596
13. $958
14. $998
15. $846
16. $658
17. $497
18. $969
19. $994
20. $787

## Page 30
1. 866
2. 892
3. 814
4. 903
5. 327
6. 762
7. 991
8. 980
9. 957
10. 866
11. 829
12. 515
13. 767
14. 305
15. 291
16. 905
17. 606
18. 940
19. 960
20. 980

## Page 31
1. $380 + $300 = $680
2. $516 + $172 = $688
3. $100 + $559 = $659
4. $612 + $100 = $712
5. 862 + 128 = 990
6. 804 + 108 = 912
7. 677 + 214 = 891
8. 385 + 508 = 893
9. 444 + 436 = 880
10. 437 + 119 = 556

## Page 32
1. 12
2. 237
3. 440
4. 102
5. 40
6. 30
7. 151
8. 57
9. 161
10. 312
11. 158
12. 203
13. 3
14. 720
15. 123
16. 111
17. 302
18. 226
19. 122
20. 581

## Page 33
1. 150
2. 431
3. 140
4. 470
5. 304
6. 612
7. 163
8. 240
9. 201
10. 123
11. 100
12. 203
13. 403
14. 22
15. 733
16. 102
17. 3
18. 350
19. 701
20. 500

*Secret Message:*
I can subtract in a flash!

## Page 34
1. 334
2. 120
3. 7
4. 545
5. 352
6. 334
7. 307
8. 309
9. 5
10. 45
11. 407
12. 423
13. 248
14. 826
15. 107
16. 241
17. 190
18. 219
19. 81
20. 592

## Page 35
*Down*
1. 90
2. 147
4. 262
5. 449
6. 483
8. 83
10. 661
11. 456
12. 49
14. 268
15. 270
16. 545

*Across*
2. 130
3. 727
6. 429
7. 698
9. 36
11. 434
13. 126
15. 280
17. 480

## Page 36
1. 60¢
2. 80¢
3. 30¢; $0.30
4. 25¢; $0.25
5. 60¢; $0.60
6. 35¢; $0.35
7. 90¢; $0.90
8. 45¢; $0.45
9. 50¢; $0.50
10. 55¢; $0.55
11. 20¢; $0.20

## Page 37
1. 75¢
2. 50¢
3. $1.00
4. $1.25
5. 30¢; $0.30
6. 70¢; $0.70
7. 80¢; $0.80
8. 60¢; $0.60
9. 75¢; $0.75
10. 100¢; $1.00
11. 65¢; $0.65
12. 50¢; $0.50
13. 40¢; $0.40

## Page 38
1. 4
2. 2
3. 7
4. 5
5. 9
6. 6
7. 10
8. 8
9. 1
10. 3
11. 3
12. 3
13. 1
14. 7
15. 2
16. 5
17. 2
18. 1
19. 2
20. 3
21. 4/5
22. 1/3
23. 2/6
24. 1/4
25. 1/2
26. 3/4
27. 6/8
28. 2/3
29. 2/5
30. 5/6

## Page 39
1. 2/4
2. 3/6
3. 2/3
4. 2/5
5. 4/6
6. 5/10
7. 4/10
8. 4/8
9. 1/3
10. 3/5
11. 2/5
12. 2/3
13. 2/4
14. 4/8
15. 3/4
16. 1/2

## Page 40
1. C
2. A
3. B
4. A
5. B
6. A
7. C
8. C
9. A
10. A
11. C
12. B
13. B
14. B
15. C

## Page 41
1. B
2. C
3. B
4. A
5. B
6. B
7. B
8. C
9. A
10. A
11. C
12. A
13. C
14. A
15. C

## Page 42
1. A
2. C
3. A
4. A
5. C
6. C
7. B
8. A
9. B
10. A
11. C
12. A
13. B
14. C
15. C

## Page 43
1. A
2. C
3. B
4. A
5. B
6. C
7. C
8. B
9. C
10. A
11. C
12. A
13. A
14. B

## Page 44
1. B
2. A
3. A
4. B
5. A
6. A
7. A
8. C
9. B
10. B
11. A
12. B
13. B
14. A
15. C

## Page 45
1. C
2. A
3. B
4. C
5. C
6. C
7. C
8. A
9. B
10. B
11. A
12. A